GARAGE SALE
SUCCESS
SECRETS

*The Definitive Step-By-Step Guide
To Turn Your Trash Into CA$H!*

Written by Garage Sale Goddess/Guru/Expert
Kathy Ozzard Chism

Edited by Sue Cruver

Inquiries should be addressed to Kathy Ozzard Chism, at kathy@kathychism.com

ISBN-13: 978-1482651928
ISBN-10: 1482651920

Library of Congress Control Number: 2013904238
LCCN Imprint Name: CreateSpace Independent Publishing Platform North Charleston, SC

Printed in the United States of America

First Printing - May 2013

**"One man's trash
is another man's treasure."**

— Tom Zart

"Simplify to simply fly."

— Kathy Ozzard Chism

DEDICATION

My mother, who passed in 1998, was a licensed antique appraiser who ran a successful antique and gift shop for many, many years in Martinsville, and later Clinton, New Jersey.

One of my favorite childhood activities was visiting garage sales on the weekends with her, discovering amazing treasures buried amongst the trash.

We also held garage sales of our own from time to time. They were always successful, and Mom taught me quite a few of the principles one needs for running them.

My mother was a sweet, kind, and gentle lady with extraordinary people skills. She lived and worked with love, thoughtfulness, and caring in whatever she did and with whomever she spoke.

She was also an accomplished artist who happened to be absolutely <u>brilliant</u> when it came to designing merchandise presentations and closing sales.

I dedicate this book to you, Mom, and thank you for all your wonderful teachings throughout my life. Although you may have not thought so at times, I was always listening.

I still am.

With Love and Gratitude, Kathy

TABLE OF CONTENTS

Dedication iv

Introduction vii

CHAPTER 1 1
Preparation, Preparation, Preparation

CHAPTER 2 11
Location, Location, Location

CHAPTER 3 21
Advertising, Advertising, Advertising

CHAPTER 4 29
Presentation, Presentation, Presentation

CHAPTER 5 37
Sell, Sell, Sell!

CHAPTER 6 45
Completion, Completion, Completion

SUCCESS! 47

BONUS TIMELINE GUIDELINE! 49

BONUS SALES SECRETS! 53

GRATITUDE 59

INTRODUCTION

I have been creating garage sales, usually one or two per year, for nearly 40 years. With many travels, educational pursuits, careers, and simply moving a lot, it has been a natural way to "clean house," earn some money, recycle, and make room each time for new possessions.

Along the way, I fine-tuned what worked and discarded what didn't. Using the same principles you will find in this book, I have consistently made nice sums of money holding garage sales in New Jersey, Virginia, Illinois, Florida, California, and Texas.

As more and more people began asking me how to do garage sales, it became evident that my knowledge needed to be shared. This book is the result. In it, I have included all the steps to succeed that I learned from my mother and from my own experiences.

Read it and refer to it the next time you want to turn your "trash into CA\$H," and discover how garage sales can be easy, fun, and profitable for anyone... including YOU!

By following the suggestions in this guide, I can almost guarantee you will make lucrative sales and be able to shift your life in new and positive ways.

Clearing out debris and what no longer works for you truly helps clear your mind as well as your home. Opening space where you live allows new energy to come in. It is a clearing on every level.

Enjoy the process, enjoy the additional money in your pocket, and enjoy new vitality – both in your home and in your life.

— Kathy

CHAPTER 1

PREPARATION, PREPARATION, PREPARATION

Where to Begin?

A <u>successful</u> garage sale is not something you create in two or three days. It takes time to prepare, and time to do it right.

First, choose a target date for your sale. This date should be at least one, and preferably two or three months out. I recommend choosing only one day instead of two for your sale, as you want to be on your best form on sale day.

Mark this date on your calendar and do not book anything for yourself to do for at least two days before the sale – not even your job. You need available time for your last minute "to-do" list before the event.

In addition, do not book anything other than something relaxing for the day after the sale, so you can "recharge your batteries."

Ideally, you want to choose a date that has a good chance for the weather to be pleasant... not too hot, not too cold, not raining, and certainly not snowing! Not easy to know months in advance, but do the best you can to align your date with predictable good weather for your area.

Good. You have picked a date.

Mark it boldly on your calendar, tell your family to mark it on theirs, say a little prayer to the weather gods, and move on to the next step.

Now, this may seem obvious, but here it is:

The more items you have for sale, the more successful your sale will be.

People love choice. Imagine going into your favorite store and there are only ten things to pick from instead of hundreds. You probably will turn around and walk out, right?

Think of your garage sale exactly like setting up a department store. The more products you have for sale, the better. The more it is presented in an attractive, easy-to-find way, the better. The cleaner your items, the better... and so on.

Most of us are amazed as we start cleaning out our closets at how much "stuff" we have accumulated through the years. Stuff we rarely use. Stuff we no longer need. Stuff that is taking up space. Stuff that someone else might really want or need.

That's the stuff you are going to put in your sale, no matter how little money you may think you will get for it, no matter how much you think it is worthless, no matter how dated it is.

People buy amazing things. I have sold little metal parts to things that I didn't have anymore and had no idea what they were for. Yet I dutifully put them in a plastic sealable bag, added a price, and they sold. I have sold extremely faded, yet clean towels to someone who needed a lot of rags for a hobby. I have sold goofy clothes from the 1980's that someone wanted for a Halloween costume.

You just never know what someone will buy, so before you throw it away, take a little time to repair it, clean it up, and sell it in your sale. Great for someone else, great for you, AND you are keeping one more item out of a landfill, which is great for our beautiful planet.

Clear Your Mind, Clear Your Space.

Before you do anything, **STOP,** and notice how you are feeling. Many people go into overwhelm just thinking about where to start to clean out their home for a garage sale, and they give up.

Don't let this be you! You are going to LOVE how it feels when you have items gone, new SPACE in your home, and MONEY in your pocket!

Before YOU go into overwhelm, give yourself three slow, deep breaths... in through your nose and out through your mouth. KNOW that it will all get done in perfect time, and you will have whatever you need to support you through the process.

Good. **Now, go get two big boxes or bins.** Mark one "Keep." Mark the other "Sell."

Start in one room at one end of your home. It is important to take everything out of a drawer, or a closet, or wherever you choose, in a systematic fashion, and **only put back what you truly want/need to keep.**

The master key to doing this right and making the most money possible is **organization.**

Say you start in your bedroom. Pull one drawer at a time out of your dresser, or nightstand, or wherever you are choosing to start. Take out an item, think about it, and then place it either in the "Keep" or "Sell" bin. If an item truly is non-salvageable, you may then <u>and only</u> <u>then</u>, throw it away. Continue this process until the drawer is completely empty.

(NOTE: You may be wondering why I haven't included a bin for Goodwill or the Salvation Army or another charity. That will come later. For now, just do the two – "Keep" and "Sell.")

If any of the items you are going to sell are dirty, broken, have threads hanging from them, need polishing, etc., take time to clean them and fix them up!

People gravitate towards things that are clean and pretty, not dirty and broken. I can't tell you how many hours I have spent in my life polishing silver, washing drinking glasses, ironing clothing – all to put in a garage sale. I can tell you that extra work has paid off in dollars, time and time again.

Once you have emptied an area and determined "Keep" or "Sell" for everything in that space, carefully put the "Keep" items back in an <u>organized</u> way. Taking the time to do this will help keep your life flowing more smoothly in the future.

Good job! Now, stand back, smile, and gaze lovingly at your accomplishment.

Reward yourself! Give yourself a little treat each time you finish an area. No, I'm not suggesting loading up on carbs, caffeine, alcohol, or sugar. Those things can reduce your energy and you need to stay energized.

Choose something like a walk outside with your dog, a Facebook break, a little yoga, or just sitting in the sun to soak in some Vitamin D. Do it for ten to twenty minutes. It will help keep your batteries charged and make the project move along faster.

OK... if you are not too tired, move on to the next area of your house to sort.

(NOTE: If you are too tired – STOP! This is not a race. This is why you are starting months in advance, so you are able to do what you can, when you can. You want to be focused and thorough, and not go into stress mode over it.)

After you complete one room, move on to the next, and repeat all the steps above. As you see and feel rooms getting clearer and cleaner, your spirits are going to begin to be lifted. You will start feeling lighter and happier. That alone is worth the effort, right?!

Remember – when you get tired, stop and come back to it later. Just do what you can do and not one thing more. Treat yourself gently, and take your time with it.

Clearing Spaces

Now a lot of people get stuck in "Oh, I might need that someday" as they are clearing spaces.

Rule of Thumb: If you haven't worn it or used it in two years, you probably never will. Unless it is a family heirloom you are saving

to hand down through generations, or something you are giving to someone else soon, or something you simply love deeply – SELL it.

Also, once you make the decision to sell something, let it go in your heart. Remember how good it is going to feel to:

+ Have the space back that it was taking up
+ Make money from it
+ Let someone else enjoy it now

Encourage other people living in your home to do the same thing. The more your family is involved in this initial clearing, the more they will want to help on sale day - especially when they know that their items will bring them their own money!

Put all items going into the sale in one location, if you can. Ideally this will be out in your garage, or in a shed, or a room that is rarely used.

Psychologically, having the items out of your most used spaces and seeing the new free space left behind makes you not want to bring any of those items back.

Items You Will Need for the Sale

To create a <u>successful</u> garage sale, you will need to purchase, rent, or borrow a number of items to advertise and present your sale properly.

I know, I know, you just want to make money, not spend it! However, it truly does take a bit of money to make money with a garage sale.

Some of these items are investments that will pay for themselves many times over as you do more sales events in the future. You can also loan or rent them out later to others who need them. (If you have friends who can loan you the larger items this first time, great.)

Here is what you will need:

+ **Sturdy display tables** of several shapes and sizes. I invested in five folding portable tables 30 years ago and have used them ever since. Occasionally, I have also used two wooden sawhorses and a huge piece of plywood to create another large, sturdy "table." The more people don't have to bend over or get near the ground to look at something, the more likely you are to sell it.

+ **Solid light color tablecloths** in the correct sizes to cover each table. This may sound silly, but having tablecloths takes your "store" up a notch, and psychologically people feel that your items are worth more. Light colors show products better than dark colors. Find tablecloths on sale at your favorite store or resale shop. Be sure they will hang down at least halfway to the ground, as well as over the front and sides of the tables.

+ **Price stickers**. Big box stores, office supply stores, certain craft shops, etc., have bright, colorful stickers with pricing like $20, $10, $5, $1, and coinage amounts pre-printed on them. Get several packages of these, as they will save you a lot of time. Get blank color stickers as well for other prices.

(continued to next page)

- **A sturdy rolling collapsible clothes rack**. You will use this not just for clothes, but also for hanging handbags, belts, and anything that shows better hanging rather than folded. ✦ **Blank price tags** with hanging threads for items where stickers won't stick, like on clothing.
- **Pens and/or permanent markers**, including one large permanent marker for your signage.
- **A portable calculator** – at least one.
- **A fanny pack** for the person at the sale dealing with the money.
- **Newspaper or tissue** to wrap breakables for your customers.
- **Empty bags** of various sizes and types for customer purchases. (Remember, think "department store.")
- **At least $10 of change in coinage and at least $30 in one and five dollar bills**. Remember the amount you put in, so you can later subtract it to determine your total profit.
- **Large and medium size neon colored sign paper** found at various big box stores, office supply stores, drug stores, craft stores, etc. You may buy pre-made garage sale signs at hardware stores, but keep in mind they tend to be too small for address reading, and they don't brand your event.
- **Small strips of wood or foam core board for each sign**. You need something to attach along the top and bottom to keep each sign straight, as humidity or morning dew will curl the paper, making it impossible to read. Make each sign the same color, so it creates "branding" for your sale.
- **Staple gun and staples**.
- **Clear packaging tape**.

✦ **Bottled water** for you and all your workers for the event. (I favor Essentia water, as it has electrolytes in it to help maintain your stamina and comes bottled in BPA-free, eco-friendly containers for recycling.)

✦ **A healthy lunch** for you and all your workers for the event.

✦ **A mirror** for people to view jewelry, clothes, etc. (Again, think "department store.") Put a sticker with "NFS" on it ("Not For Sale") on the mirror and anything else you are keeping that people may see and want to buy.

✦ One or two **jewelry organizers** for inside drawers if you are selling jewelry. These have quite a few compartments for displaying your pieces, and separates them all quite nicely.

✦ **Electrical extension cords** for anything electronic to prove it works... and a place to plug them in.

✦ **A "boom box"** or something to play soft music on, particularly if you are selling CDs.

✦ **Large, inexpensive, clear plastic paint drop cloths** – enough to cover your tables and items in case it rains. (These are easy to find at paint or hardware stores.)

✦ **Working batteries** for any small electronics so people may test them.

✦ **Baskets in various sizes** for grouping items, such as pet toys, or hair scrunchies, or screwdrivers, or whatever.

✦ **Layered clothing and comfortable shoes.** Suggest this to your helpers as well. You will all be standing most of the day and the temperatures will undoubtedly shift. Each person will also want a hat and sunglasses available to wear, if needed.

✦ **A couple of folding chairs or stools** if someone needs to sit down.

(Note: If your sale is at a community event location, find out what items are provided before investing in the above, and only purchase or borrow the rest.)

CHAPTER 2

LOCATION, LOCATION, LOCATION

Decide Where and Who

It is very important that you choose a great location for your sale. You want a place that is easy to find, well populated, has plenty of parking, is safe, and the neighbors don't mind. You also want to be sure garage sales are legal in the area you choose, and if you need a permit to hold your event.

My favorite place to hold garage sales was when I lived on a cul-de-sac, right off of a fairly busy street. There was plenty of parking available in front of my neighbor's houses, and I always checked with them first to see if they had any concerns about my upcoming event. It is important to be considerate of your neighbors, as they will be there long after your buyers leave.

About a month before my sale date, I make up a little flyer about the sale, and invite all my neighbors to participate at their homes, too, if they so wish.

There are several advantages to this:

1. More people involved means sharing the cost of advertising.
2. Garage sale customers love to go to areas where they may park and shop at many homes, instead of driving all over town.
3. It lends a festive air to the day and improves neighbor relations by letting them know ahead of time what is about to happen.

I have also been known to invite my friends to participate as well. All they needed to do was bring a table or two and set up on the street near me. Again, the more, the merrier.

You may be thinking that more people selling will mean fewer sales for you. It is actually quite the opposite. When others are involved, they are going to tell all their friends about the event, as well as help advertise it. This brings more people to the event - hence, more sales.

(NOTE: Due to the fact that I take the time to present my items like a store, I consistently sell more than anyone else. I have never made less than $400 at any of my garage sales, usually make between $800 - $1200 after expenses, and at times have made over $2,000 in less than eight hours! Twenty-five cents here, $1 there, $5 here, $20 there... it really <u>does</u> add up.)

Share Your Workload

Whether you choose to do a group "street sale" or a sale on your own, you are going to need help. You simply can't spend all day outside without taking a few breaks, and you can't possibly watch everyone at all times.

Although I have usually found people who visit garage sales to be kind and trustworthy, sadly, you may have something stolen from your sale if you don't have extra pairs of eyes watching the "customers."

This happens rarely, yet feels awful when it does. Instead of getting angry, I decided long ago if someone has to steal from a garage sale, they must be desperate. So I silently bless them, wish them well, and I don't hang on to the upset.

How Much Help?

Depending on the size of your sale, you will need at least one other person to help you. I usually have two to three extra helpers, especially in the first few hours when more customers show up. I always provide some healthy food and water for them.

Something interesting often happens with helpers. Have you known people who work in a clothing store and find they are spending a lot of their paychecks on clothes? Hanging around something attractive and desirable all day long gives them the "I wants."

The same happens with helpers at a garage or yard sale. They start thinking of all sorts of reasons why they need something they see on one of your tables. They put it aside and offer to pay you at the end of the day.

More often than not, he or she chooses a lot of things and sometimes becomes your best customer of the day. Since they have been kind enough to help, I always add everything up that they want, give them a special price for all of it, and then offer anything left at the end of the sale to them for free.

Everyone goes home happy at my sales, including me!

Best Dates, Times, and Pricing

Through the years, I have found Fridays and Saturdays to be the best days for garage sales. Fridays are interesting because a lot of people will stop by before they go to work. These same people may not come out on a weekend because they are too busy doing other things with their families.

Something you have probably heard, but need to hear again, is that you simply can't stop the "early birds." These are people who live for garage sales. They are often antique, art, or jewelry dealers looking for special finds. They will show up WAY before you are set up and ready, hoping to be the first ones to see your wares.

I usually set my "open" times from 9:00AM – 4:00PM, and tell people in my advertising and in person that from 2:00PM on, all items left will be half price from what is marked.

On the day of the sale, I wake up ridiculously early and am out setting up by 6:30AM – knowing the early birds will start arriving at 7:00AM, and sometimes earlier!

I used to get really, really annoyed by this. However, at some point I decided to embrace it, as these truly will be some of your best customers if they like what you have.

To handle the inconvenience, I learned over the years to ask at least two helpers to be with me at these early times, so they may help me set up the tables, get the items onto the tables, and keep setting up as I help these eager shoppers.

Getting Ready for the Sale

More on actual sale day later. For now, let's focus on getting ready for the sale.

You want to price EVERYTHING with stickers or hanging tags ahead of time. Yes, everything. Just like in a store, this makes it easy for customers to see if a price for something is even in their range, and you will not have your sale day constantly interrupted with questions about prices.

Make your prices easy to read and choose prices that are realistic.

Pricing Guidelines

At garage sales you will never get what you originally paid for an item, even if it is brand new and still in the box. With most items you will get less than half of its original value. If you have an item or items that have significant value, sell them on places like Craigslist or eBay instead.

Having said that, my sister and I held a yard sale at our mother's home several months after she passed, and actually sold her van at the sale for thousands of dollars! You truly just never know.

(As an aside, most items are non-taxable at garage sales because you are selling them for less than what you paid for them, so there are no capital gains. However, if you sell something for more than what you paid for it, you <u>are</u> required to pay taxes, and if you hold more than two or three garage sales per year, you may be required to get a business license. Check with the rules in your area about such things.)

In pricing items, keep in mind that most people will want to ask you for a better price than on the tag. Therefore, make your prices a wee bit more than what you will actually accept, and still be willing to take less if needed.

Try to recall what you paid for each item, or find the original receipt. This will help give you a starting point for your pricing. Remember, at a garage sale you will rarely get more than half of what you originally paid for an item, and usually less... often far less.

Every region of the country is different, and every neighborhood is different, so it is impossible to have "rules" around pricing. Then there is the fact that two of the exact same items get handled differently though the years by different owners, so wear and tear will not be the same.

However, I will do my best to give you a few ideas for how to price your items based on my experiences with this in various states. **In all of the cases below, I am assuming the items are clean, attractive, working perfectly, and not in any need of repair.**

- ✦ **Computers, televisions, cameras, and most electronics** sell very well, if current. Price them at one quarter to one third of their original value. If the item is already out of date, however, you will get little for it, unless it is very collectible. I had to sell a $250 medium sized stereo system for $20 after the iPods and their cute little speaker systems came out... and I was probably lucky to get that.
- ✦ If you have **antiques**, you are usually far better off selling those on eBay or Craigslist, or at a consignment shop. However, if you want to try to sell them at your sale, check on eBay or Craigslist for the prices of items like yours to get ideas for what you should charge.

✦ **Art** is subjective. If it is of some value, follow the same rules as for antiques above. Otherwise, price it for what you think it is worth, and if you know something about the artist, be sure to include that either typed up and taped to the back of the piece, or speak about it to interested customers on sale day.

✦ Standard **clothing** almost never sells. If your clothes have some value, take them to a resale shop instead. I have made lots of money over the years from resale shops, and very little at my garage sales with clothing. I usually wind up taking most items to Goodwill or the Salvation Army after the sale. However, shoes, coats, handbags, scarves, hats, gloves, and other accessories usually do well. You won't get much money for any of them, but they will most probably sell. I usually price shoes between $5 - $10 per pair, coats for $10 - $20 depending on the quality, and accessories in the $2 - $10 range. Again, if items from your closet are really worth something, take them to a resale shop instead. It is also a good idea to group things together – like socks, for example. Throw them all into a large plastic sealable bag, put a price on it like $5, and sell them as one item.

✦ **Tools, vacuum cleaners, appliances, clocks, and all kitchen items** sell really, really well. Price these at one third to one half of their original value.

✦ **Bicycles, automotive supplies, and most sporting goods** sell very well. You will want to price these at one third to one half of their original value. If someone wants to take a bicycle for a test ride in your neighborhood, only let them if they leave their driver's license or something else they really need as collateral. Never let a customer take an item away from your sale to show someone else before deciding to buy, even if they leave a down-payment. You may never see it again.

- **China and glassware** sell well. Sell these at one quarter of their original value.
- **Furniture, area rugs, and lamps** also sell extremely well, if they are in good, clean, working condition. Arrange furniture into attractive "room" settings in your driveway. To help keep anyone other than serious buyers from sitting on the items, I make "tent" signs with words like "Sofa - $300" on them, and place them on the furniture. That way, if a sign gets moved, even your helpers will know where it belongs. Painter's tape works well on most surfaces to help keep signs from blowing away in a wind. Plug in lamps so people may turn them on and see them work. Price your furniture, area rugs, and lamps between one quarter to one half of their original values.
- In my experience, **jewelry and watches** are usually the first things to sell. There are people who go to garage sales, usually dealers, usually as "earlybirds," who specifically look for these two items... and they only want gold, silver, or platinum. Follow the antiques rules for your better watches and pieces of jewelry. With costume jewelry, I usually price earrings at $2-$4 a pair, necklaces at $5-$10, bracelets at $3-$5, and watches at $5-$10 each. Again, have a mirror available for people to see how these items will look, keep a pair of eyes on the jewelry table at all times as that is where the most items get stolen, and invest in little jewelry drawer organizers to use for displaying pieces so they stay separated.
- **Garden items, lawn equipment, and potted plants** sell very well, too. Price them at one quarter to one third of their original value.
- **Books**, sadly, do not sell well. If you have high quality coffee table books, find a book consignment shop for them instead. If you have a book signed by the author, sell it on a site like Craigslist or eBay. Otherwise, price paperbacks

between 25 cents to $2, and hardbacks from 50 cents to $5. Know that you will probably donate most of them to a library after the sale.

+ **Clean bedding, linens, towels, placemats, etc.**, all sell well – at low prices. Price them in the 50 cent to $20 range, depending on quality and size. (For example, $20 for a bed comforter and pillow sham set, 50 cents for a washcloth.)

+ **Pet items** sell well, too, at low prices. Be sure to wash all bedding, crates, pet clothing, dishes, toys, etc., before selling them. Most of these sell between 50 cents to $20 each, depending on the item.

+ **Office supplies** sell very well. Price them at one quarter to one half of their original value. Combine matching papers and envelopes into bags and sell as one item. Remember to display your items like a high-end store would. (Think "merchandising, merchandising, merchandising!") If you are selling a pen holder, put some pens in it. If you are selling a stamp holder, put a couple of stamps in it so a customer knows what it is.

+ **CDs and DVDs** sell well, at least at this printing, priced at $1-$2 per CD, $2-$5 per DVD. Years ago, VHS tapes sold well - now they don't sell at all. The same will be true one day for CDs and DVDs, so sell them now if you are thinking about reducing your collections.

+ **Holiday decorations** sell well, particularly if nearing the holiday. If you are selling Christmas ornaments and have a "fake" Christmas tree, use it to display them, and tag every ornament with a price. These will sell better from August through December, rather than the rest of the year. Fourth of July decorations sell better between May through July. You get the idea. Remember to group holiday items together per holiday on your tables. Price them at one quarter of their original price.

✦ **Musical instruments** sell very well, but you will usually want to sell these on Craigslist, eBay, etc. Be sure to check these places for current realistic prices if you do choose to sell them in your garage sale.

✦ Last, but certainly not least, **children's toys, games, and clothing** all sell well. Not for much money, but they will sell. Remember, a little here and a little there really adds up. Price these items at one quarter of what you originally paid for them.

If you need more help, feel free to comment on my Garage Sale Success Secrets Facebook page, and our community there will help you as best we can. Don't be discouraged if a customer tells you that your prices are too high. I hear it at nearly every sale. I still sell like crazy.

However, don't get greedy. If somebody offers you something, and it is not too low, take it. You have only a few hours to sell a lot of things, and you have no guarantees anyone else will come along and want that item.

Remember, your goal is to get rid of these goods, not hang on to them forever. The bottom line is that if you have decided to sell it, it is now worth what someone else is willing to pay for it.

Yes, pricing everything before the sale takes a lot of time, but make the time to do it. It will pay off on the day of the sale, and you will be glad you did.

Remember, you are reading this book to become a Garage Sale Queen or King, not a Garage Sale Pauper!

CHAPTER 3

ADVERTISING, ADVERTISING, ADVERTISING

Get the Word Out

About two weeks before your sale, call your local paper and place an ad. If your sale is on a Saturday, place the ad for Thursday, Friday, and Saturday. If your sale is on a Friday, place the ad for Thursday and Friday.

It will cost some money, yet it is well worth the price to drive traffic to your sale. Make sure your ad will run in the "real" paper and online. The staff at the paper is usually fantastic in helping you design your ad, guiding you on how to word it, what to put in bold print, etc.

Here is a sample of a newspaper street sale ad my neighbors and I did a couple of years ago:

HUGE STREET SALE
TO BENEFIT ANIMAL RESCUE!
(www.dreamoneworld.org)
7 Homes, 1 cul-de-sac!
CASH ONLY, NO $100's, Pay Per House.

Enter to Win $20 Gas Card!!!
Form signed at all 7 homes to be eligible.
Antiques, Art, Automotive, Books,
Cameras, Candles/Holders, Car Seat,
CDs, China, Clothing, Coolers,
Copper Ship, Christmas Tree/Decor,
Duo-matic 80 Knitting Machine, DVDs,
Electronics, Frames, Furn., Glass,
Hot Wheels Cars, Gary Fisher Bike,
Hsld. Items, Kitchen and Laundry Appliances,
Jewelry, Lamps, Linens, Luggage,
Office Supplies, Pet Items, Rugs, Tools,
Tree Gaffs, Toys, Yoga Items, etc.
(My Address)
Sat 9-4

Some things to note about this ad...

1. This sale was a benefit for animal rescue. When you add a charitable purpose, more people will be inclined to come to your sale over others in your neighborhood. In this case, each neighbor chose what percentage they wanted to donate. In some cases it was 100%, in others 20%, in others 10% - all donations were gratefully accepted.
2. We alphabetized the main items for sale, to make it easier for people to read and remember.
3. We purposely mentioned high quality, big, or highly unusual items to attract collectors.
4. As we had seven families involved and all were sharing the cost of advertising, one of my neighbors came up with a great idea of offering a $20 gas card for someone to win. We all pitched in to purchase it. I made up little forms for names and phone numbers and/or email addresses, which we all handed out to customers. They had to get each home to initial their form in order

to be eligible. This meant they would see everyone's items on the street. Brilliant! At the end of the day, the forms went into a hat. A winner was chosen, contacted, and the gas card was sent.

(NOTE: I only recommend doing something like this if a lot of people are involved, as it adds extra work to the day. However, along with the charity kindness, it was a great draw for bringing people to our sale vs. several other large street sales that were happening nearby!)

5. You will notice that we advertised and required cash only, and no $100 bills. Even though we always want to trust people, I have had too many checks bounce through the years, so now have a policy of cash only. I recommend only taking checks if you know the individual personally. As it is difficult to make change if people give you $100 bills, I rule those out, too.

With the proliferation of ATM machines, people can usually get the cash for you rather easily. If they ask me to hold items while they get the funds needed, I give them a short window of time, and have them give me something as collateral or a small down-payment until they return. Otherwise, they may never return, and you have taken items to sell out of your "store" for no reason. If they can't leave something as collateral, I explain kindly that I have to leave the items on display and urge them to return quickly. They always do.

More on Advertising

You have called your local paper and placed an ad. About six or seven days before your sale, create a **Facebook event** if you use Facebook. If you don't, get someone who does use Facebook to create the event for you. Facebook is a wonderful way to get the word out. Ask your friends to pass the event link on to their friends, too.

(NOTE: If you create the event or advertise too far in advance, people will forget about it. You want to give them enough time to plan for it, yet close enough to the event so they don't forget.)

Email all your local friends with a little **online flyer** you create, and ask them to pass that on, too.

Be concise, yet include details in your information. List the date, time, location, list of items for sale, and other relevant information like the newspaper ad mentioned above.

Use **free online advertising sources**. We are so fortunate to live in a day and age where so many free options are available!

For example, **Craigslist** is a HUGE advertiser for garage sales. I often ask customers how they heard about my sale, and an average of 50% say Craigslist.

There will often be other **local free online groups** where you can advertise. Ask around and then use them. The more you get the word out there, the more people you will have at your event.

Signage

Have you ever driven down a street and seen little signs that say "Garage Sale," but there is no way to read the tiny date, time, or address?

You want your street signage to be a decent size, easy to read, and legible, so it will bring customers to your sale. Here are some tips:

1. Use bright, neon, and light colors, like yellow, orange, and pink for the paper. Ideally, keep all your signs the same color for consistency and "branding."

2. Write in big, bold, black permanent ink. Keep it concise, make it easy to read, use nice handwriting, and get to the point:

Saturday, 8/15
HUGE GARAGE SALE!
123 Main Street
9AM - 4PM

Signage is not the place to get wordy. You want people in cars traveling at speeds to be able to read them at a glance. You also want the signs to somewhat professional. It may sound trivial, but nicer signs bring in more people.

You also want to leave space below the wording and along the sides to draw BIG arrows in whatever direction you want them to go, depending on where you are placing the signs. You will draw in these big, thick arrows with a BIG magic marker just before putting each one up.

The night before the sale, I drive around my area after dark when there is little traffic. I use either a staple gun for wooden poles, or clear packaging tape for metal poles, to place my signs. I recommend doing this with a friend or family member for safety reasons.

Again, condensation through the night will "wilt" and curl the paper. To prevent that from happening, attach something from end to end across the top and across the bottom to keep each sign taut. I like to use a 1-inch strip of wood or some foam core board.

(NOTE: Please first be sure your county, city, and local community all allow signage to be attached to poles and street signs. Some do, and some do not.)

The same night after your sale, or at the very latest the next day, please be sure to take all your signs down as a courtesy to other folks who might need to use the space and for the sake of our planet. Otherwise, it just becomes litter!

As I usually am the one to organize the group street sale, I walk the street and place a flyer I make at everyone's front door about five weeks before the possible date choice. This gives everyone plenty of time to respond and plan his or her schedule accordingly. Then I give follow-up calls to those who have agreed to participate, tell them the chosen date, give them some tips for sale day, etc.

Again, a neighborhood garage sale is a great way to get to know your neighbors better, and it can be a fun community event!

For those doing a group sale, on the following page is a sample flyer.

Hi, (my street)! It's me, Kathy Chism again, from (my street address), and we are planning our **2ⁿᵈ Annual Dream One World Street Sale for Animal Rescue**, as the first one was such a great success!!! Please choose the Saturday date below you prefer, and the one with the most will be the one we use. The event will be from 9AM – 4PM.

If you have more items you would like to sell, this is a great way to do it... and if you have any friends that would like to set up a table or two with you and sell some things as well, that will be wonderful, too. The more money we raise, the better! ☺

Again, once the sale is finished, you decide what amount you would like to donate from your proceeds to Dream One World towards our animal rescue work, and you will receive a tax deductible donation for that amount. It's a win-win for everyone!

We assist one rescue for cats (Feline Rescue of Northern California), one rescue for dogs (Rainbow Rescue), and one for horses (Change). All of these are small, from-the-heart nonprofits that <u>always</u> need help with fundraising as they are so busy getting the rescued animals their shots, grooming, food, medicines, etc.

Believe me, they are all so grateful for whatever funding we create for them!

Please return the bottom of this sheet to me in the bag at our front door (NOT our mailbox, please!) or call me **no later than Wednesday, July 7**, so I may start working on the creation and promotion of the day. We will all share again in the promotion costs, which are not large, especially if many people participate.

I look forward to hearing from all of you and sharing this day with you!

With Gratitude,
Kathy Chism (my phone number)
Founder/Director
Dream One World, Inc.
www.dreamoneworld.org (Read more about the rescues we assist on our website!)

Please cut here and return bottom portion... Thank you!

_____

_____'____ Yes! Please count me/us in for this event! Name(s) _____

_____ Address: _____ Phone: _____

_____ No. Sadly, I can't participate this year... Name(s) _____

_____ Address: _____ Phone: _____

Preferred Date: August 7 _____ August 14 _____ August 21 _____ August 28 _____

CHAPTER 4

PRESENTATION, PRESENTATION, PRESENTATION

Two or Three Days Before Your Sale

1. Price everything if you haven't already.
2. If you have a garage, put your cars out in your driveway or on the street if it is safe to do so, so you may use your garage as a staging area. Please don't block anyone's mailbox or walkway. We want to be good neighbors at all times.
3. Iron all your tablecloths. Set up the tables and put the cloths on them.
4. Since on the morning of the sale you will want to open your garage door and bring the tables out and set them up exactly as planned for your driveway or street, set your tables up inside the garage that way. Keep more expensive and/or breakable items, like jewelry or fine glassware, on tables closest to where you will be standing during the sale. Usually this is just inside or outside your garage door.
5. Group items together in attractive displays. One table may be for kitchen items, another for electronics, another for holiday items, another for linens, or office supplies, or pet items, or whatever. Think "store." Just as you don't find clothing on the crystal tables

at Macy's, don't do it at your garage sale either. (See photos at the end of this chapter for display table ideas.)

6. If you have electronics that have remote controls and/or other pieces, be sure to put all these extra bits into one Ziploc bag, and mark the bag as part of the item that goes with it all. If you have the original instruction booklets for any items, be sure to include these. If you have an original sales receipt to prove how much you paid for an item, have it ready as this can come in handy from time to time.

7. Make sure you have a little table or storage ledge near where you will be standing during the sale with a few pens, a calculator, blank pricing labels, bags, wrapping papers or bubble wrap for your customers, and some folding chairs for you and your helpers.

8. Make your signs if you haven't already. Be sure to make a huge one that says, "Most items 1/2 OFF between 2PM – 4PM." I like to use a large piece of foam core board for this, using a giant black permanent marker.

By preparing two or three days before your sale day, you are not running around like a crazy person the day before, trying to get it all done at once. You need to be rested before the event.

Preparing ahead gives you extra time, if needed, to finish setting up with grace and ease instead of with stress and frenzy.

The Day and Night Before Your Sale

1. If there is something left from the previous day's lists, finish it.
2. Call your helpers and remind them of the time you need them to be at your event site. Tell them you will have food and water for them. Explain that you will be handling all the money to keep things simple, and to please direct customers to you when they are ready to pay. Also explain that when a customer is there, it is

not the time to be chatting with you or other helpers. Instead, everyone must be focused on customer needs just as if working at a department store. Thank them again profusely for being willing to help.

3. Get or prepare the food for you and your helpers. Choose things that are not messy, are easy to eat, and will still taste good later if you get interrupted by customers.

4. If you still need to get change in coins and bills from the bank for your sale, go do it.

5. Take some time off just for you today, relaxing as much as you can. You need to store up your energy for tomorrow.

6. Choose a time, usually after dark, to go with your friend or family member to place your signs around your neighborhood. Together you will be safer, and the task will go much faster.

Place your signs around the same height as a stop sign – the height where drivers can see them and read them better as they drive by. Be sure to put signs well ahead of the turn to your location, so drivers may get in the correct lane and be prepared to make the turn. Put a sign at the turn as well, so they know they are in the right place.

Signage is very important. In placing signs, think of where most of your traffic will come from. Identify good landmarks and give drivers ample time to slow down and turn when needed to get to your sale. I usually put up between 12-16 signs around my area at a number of local intersections.

7. Eat a good, healthy dinner the night before the sale and try to get to bed early. You are going to be getting up early, and you want to be well rested.

CHAPTER 5

SELL, SELL, SELL!

From Event Planner to Salesperson

You have spent weeks and weeks preparing for this day. You have cleaned out your closets, created a small department store, done advertising for your Big Day, and it is finally here.

SHOWTIME!

As quickly as you can and with as much help as is available, get those tables out at least two hours before your sale officially starts. Lay breakables down flat before moving the laden tables. Finish placing your items the way you want them.

This is the one time of the day when you may feel a bit rushed, and with good reason. The earlybirds are coming!

Remember to breathe deep breaths. Delegate to helpers what is needed, and explain that this is the part of the day where they are really going to need to hurry.

Then, when all is out and ready, it is time for you to become a salesperson.

"What?! I thought I could just sort and clean and price everything, set it out, and then count change for people as they bring me their money!"

Well, this can work to a certain degree, but to hold a really <u>successful</u> garage sale, you must engage with your customers all day long.

Now, you may be thinking you are a "terrible" salesperson, or not one at all. Let go of those thoughts right now. **You have been successfully selling all your life.**

If you recommended a product to someone and they tried it, you were a successful salesperson for that company, even though you weren't paid.

Any time you have been hired, you had to successfully "sell" yourself to your employer.

When you nudge your children to do something good, you are selling them on the benefits of why they should do it.

If you have a partner, you "sold" them on your fabulous personal attributes.

So be confident! You have sales ability, and once people start buying from you, you will enjoy the sales process.

Having been in sales off and on for many years, I can tell you that truly great salespeople simply communicate from their hearts, tell the truth, know their product, sell items they love, and give buyers permission to purchase something they actually really want and/or need.

At the end of this book is a BONUS section with secrets for those who want to take their salesmanship skills to a higher level. For now, here are some simple, easy tips to help you sell at your event:

1. <u>Smile</u> and sincerely greet everyone as they arrive. Look people in their eyes with your smiling eyes. Treat them as though they are guests in your home. Suggest they please ask you if they have any questions. If you see them looking quizzically at something, gently go over and explain what it is and how it works.

Encourage them to sit in furniture if you have any, try on jewelry and look in the mirror, offer to play a track from a CD they seem interested in it, and so on.

Engage with them, help them, yet don't hang around them. Let them look first and after a helpful phrase or two, move back to let them look on their own some more.

2. Have you ever been in a department store with a number of items you want to purchase that you have to carry around? They get heavy after a while, your hands are full, and you find you are taking less and less interest in shopping.

Remember <u>that</u> when you see someone at your sale carrying around one or two items in his or her hands, and offer to put those items in a safe space until they are finished shopping. This encourages them to shop more, and more, and more.

3. Please don't eat in front of customers, don't play with or talk on your cell phone in front of customers, and don't discuss personal things with your helpers in front of customers. In other words, pretend you are at work at a high-end department store, being paid 100% commission, and your job is to be extremely

professional, knowledgeable, kind, engaging, and helpful to every single customer.

Yes, it is a driveway or a street, and it is "just a garage sale." However, if you <u>really</u> want to make the most money possible, you must treat it like a job, and give your customers the utmost respect and attention.

4. Certain things may happen during the day that can make your sales suffer.

I have had helpers who don't realize all the time and energy and money you have put into making this day happen, and simply want to chat with you all day long.

This is why I suggest you tell them up front that when a customer is around, you simply can't do that, as you need to focus on the event. Tell them you will love chatting with them another day.

Then there can be customers that want to chat and tell you really long stories about something, not realizing that you have only a few hours to get everything in your driveway sold. Excuse yourself from these conversations in a kind manner, and move on to help another customer.

Conversations about anything other than the items presented can be distracting for customers, and we want them all to stay focused. I also always play a little soft new age music in the background so that the space feels more welcoming and serene.

5. Then, there may be the weather to shift your plans. One year I did a yard sale along a busy street with a dear friend at her home in Miami, and the skies opened up and poured with rain about two hours into the sale. Yikes!

Fortunately, we had our big, thin, inexpensive plastic paint drop cloths available, and we quickly covered everything with them, pulling them tight so drivers could still see our items.

For the next hour while it poured, we stood out there in our raincoats and literally had drive-by shopping! People would pull up, roll down their windows a little bit and shout things like, "How much for the candle holder?"

We sold an amazing amount of items shouting out prices in the deafening rain, grabbing things out from under the drop cloths, and exchanging items for money through car windows!

6. Speaking of weather, note that the sun can bake certain items in a destructive way, or make metal objects very hot to the touch. You don't want to leave things like candles, old record albums, and other things that melt out in the sun. You also need a backup plan if the wind picks up. Be ready to weight items down if need be.

7. As more and more of your items get sold, consolidate, consolidate, consolidate. Keep arranging things so your tables constantly look attractive and "full."

Again, think department store. Things are always nicer to go through if they are not messy, mixed up, or in the wrong place. Customers will often pick something up, carry it around for a little while, and then put it down somewhere else.

I rarely sit down during a garage sale, as I am either assisting customers or keeping my tables organized and attractive.

When you sell out of a number of items, it is time to take down one or more of the tables so that your other tables remain full instead of sparse. As you remove tables, keep the others near each other so it still looks like a "store."

You also want to be sure that people see some of your items at all times as they drive down your street. If everything is up close to your home, you may lose some customers as they don't see much and think your sale is already over or "all the good stuff is probably gone already."

Sometimes I get helium balloons the day before the sale and tie them to a light at the end of my driveway, or my mailbox. This helps people find your sale, and lets them know it is still going on even when the pickings get slimmer.

8. Be sure to drink plenty of pure water throughout the day to stay hydrated. It is said one should drink 1/2 their body weight in ounces daily, and even more when in the sun.

For example, someone weighing 120 lbs. would need 60 ounces daily, and more when exercising or spending time in the sun. Keep plenty of good water on hand, and drink it. It will help give you energy, too.

9. Throughout the sale I mention to people that the prices will be half price from 2:00PM – 4:00PM, just in case they didn't see my sign. Inevitably, one, two, or more do come back, and even with these few numbers, I have had some great sales that I wouldn't have had otherwise by doing this.

Most, however, do not come back, so you want to explain the half price rule as a real bonus to everyone who does show up during that final time period.

You are nearing the end of your sale by this time. You need to sell as much as you can, so don't get hung up on how much the item was originally worth or that it seems like such a shame to let it go for so little. Something is better than nothing.

10. Your "fanny pack" is your cash register. Wear it all day long, as you do not want to set it down and have someone leave with it. Throughout the day, as you take in more and more money, I suggest taking the bills that are $10 and higher out every hour or so and putting them in a safe place indoors. Leave just enough in your fanny pack to easily make change.

11. A word about food, children, and dogs. I love all three. However, I have had little chocolate covered fingers touch clothing for sale, a little male dog lifting his leg and peeing on an upholstered chair for sale, a big dog happily wagging her tail and knocking over a slew of items on a table, etc. You have permission to gently ask customers to please keep their children and pets away from your items. Most department stores would do the same.

CHAPTER 6

COMPLETION, COMPLETION, COMPLETION

Whew! My Sale is Over! Now What?

It's 4:00PM and time to start packing up, unless you still have customers.

By now you are probably more than a little tired. Have any helpers who are left assist you in getting items back into your garage or a neutral place. **Try not to bring them back into your home.**

Settle up with any purchases your helpers want to make, and offer any leftover items to them for free.

Have them help you fold up and store your empty tables.

Thank them profusely, give them a big hug, and send them home.

If your energy is depleted, leave the rest for later or tomorrow, and go relax.

When you feel ready, get two boxes. One is for the charity of your choice. The other is for items left over that you are going to try to sell on Craigslist or eBay, or give to friends.

Again, **try not to bring anything back into your home,** unless you have truly changed your mind about an item and feel joy in your heart that it didn't sell.

As soon as you safely can, go take your signs down.

Then, soak your feet.

Oh, yes... and count your money. ☺

SUCCESS!

CONGRATULATIONS!

You did it! Great job! I am so proud of you!!!

Now YOU are a garage sale pro, too.

By taking your time, staying organized, enlisting help, using lots of advertising, being prepared for any situation, presenting your wares in a beautiful way, being a caring salesperson, and staying upbeat yet calm throughout the entire process – you had a very successful garage sale!

Congratulate yourself for being willing to release the stuff in your life you no longer needed. You should feel freer, more organized, more prosperous, more empowered, and happier as a result of your success.

Feels good, doesn't it?!

I invite you to join my GSSS Facebook page and offer any tips, suggestions, ideas, and joys from your garage sale experience to share with others! https://www.facebook.com/garagesalesuccesssecrets

Now, start planning for that next great sale and let me know how it goes.
Happy selling!

With Love and Gratitude, Kathy ♥♥♥

BONUS TIMELINE GUIDELINE!

Here is a handy reference tool to keep nearby once you have read this book from start to finish. It will help remind you of actions to take along the way as you prepare for your successful sale!

A

TWO TO THREE MONTHS BEFORE THE SALE:

1. Choose a date, preferably on a Friday or a Saturday.
2. Begin clearing your home with two boxes or bins marked "Keep" and "Sell."
3. Clean, repair, polish, sew, iron, etc. - all items that need cleaning and/or repair.
4. Purchase items you need for the sale - see complete list in Chapter 1.
5. Choose a location for your sale, and invite any neighbors, family, and/or friends who may want to participate to join you.
6. Enlist at least one helper for your sale, and preferably two or more.
7. Begin pricing your items.

B

TWO WEEKS BEFORE YOUR SALE:

1. Place ad with local newspaper - both the paper version and online.
2. Create your signage.
3. Continue with any items from **"A"** not completed yet.

C

ONE WEEK BEFORE YOUR SALE:

1. Create a Facebook event about your sale.
2. Advertise on Craigslist and other free online forums.
3. Create an online flyer about your event, and email it to all your local friends and family. Tell them to pass it on to whoever they think may be interested, too.
4. If creating a group sale, check in with other participants to see if they have any questions, to offer advice, and to go over details of the day.

D

TWO TO THREE DAYS BEFORE YOUR SALE:

1. Finish pricing all your items.
2. Iron all your tablecloths for the event.
3. Set up all your tables in a "holding area," and put the table cloths on them.
4. Group items on your tables.
5. Get change in coins and small bills from the bank.
6. Complete everything in "A," "B," and "C."

E

THE DAY AND NIGHT BEFORE YOUR SALE:

1. Finish everything in "D."
2. Call your helpers to remind them of the time you need them to show up for your event, and the other items for them listed in Chapter 4.
3. Get or prepare the food for you and your helpers.
4. Take some time to relax and charge up <u>your</u> batteries.
5. After dark, take a friend with you and hang your signage around your neighborhood.
6. Eat a healthy dinner, and get to bed early. Sleep well! You have done all you can do, and you are now ready to have a fantastic, successful sale day tomorrow!

F

SALE DAY:

1. Wake up early, stretch, and know it is going to be a wonderful, successful, and fun day.
2. Eat a healthy breakfast.
3. Two hours before your sale "officially starts," get your tables out and complete your setup.
4. Hug your helpers when they arrive. Have water and a little snack ready for them.
5. Start selling! Follow the suggestions in Chapter 5 as well as the Bonus sales tips.
6. Remember to periodically secure larger bills in a safe space inside your home.
7. At the end of the sale, bring leftover items inside, and take down your tables.

8. Hug your helpers again, thank them profusely, have them pay for their purchases, give them some unsold items they like for free, and send them home.
9. Rest. Soak your feet.
10. When you have enough energy, decide which unsold items you are going to give to charity, sell online, give to friends and family, throw away, or keep for your next sale.
11. Take down your neighborhood signs.
12. Count your money. ☺

GOOD JOB!

Congratulate yourself on running a truly <u>successful</u> garage sale!

BONUS SALES SECRETS!

As a special thank you for purchasing this book, to follow is a shortened version of some "languaging" **secrets** most people are taught when they go through sales training with big corporations.

Different people "speak" different "languages." You already know that if you travel to Japan and speak English to someone who only speaks Japanese, it will be nearly impossible for he or she to understand you.

Once you speak in their language, however, even if you are not proficient at it, they will warm up to you immediately, and will make every effort to understand you.

In selling, you must speak at least four languages. There are many terms for it, but I learned it as the "DESA" system. These are not "tricks" - merely lessons in better communication with our fellow brothers and sisters on this earth.

People tend to fall into one of four categories:

Dominant

Expressive

Solid

Analytical

Yes, some will be a combination of two or three, or even all four, but you will usually very quickly be able to see one category being more pronounced than the others.

1. A **"Dominant"** person hates wasting time, knows a bit about what he or she is looking for, wants to be in control of the situation and really doesn't want much, if any, input from the salesperson, feels they know everything about an item already, is usually in a hurry, and has little patience. They may not even look at you or respond to you when you speak to them.

This is not a person who will want to engage in conversation. You simply tell this person you are available if they have any questions, and other than your smile and initial greeting, you usually only engage with them if they engage with you. Be a good listener when they do, and keep your answers or suggestions succinct, intelligent, and to the point, in a calm, sure voice.

Interestingly, these people tend to be very loyal to salespeople they like. If they feel respected, they may stick around longer than planned. I often find myself just naturally saying "Yes, Sir," or "Yes, Ma'am" to Dominants. These people usually have money to spend, and will spend it easily, as they make decisions quickly.

2. An **"Expressive"** person is just that – expressive! They will be very effusive and excited about what they are seeing, loving colors or the wonders of an item, tending to use hand gestures, laughing, chatting away, wanting to tell you stories... and they may have short attention spans.

Speak to them in their language – agreeing with the beauty and "fabulousness" of an item, being excited in your speech, looking them in the eyes with plenty of smiles, and using a few hand gestures of your own. Don't go into details about how something works unless they ask. They are attracted to the beauty of an item, not its practical side.

These are fun people, so be careful, as you can easily get drawn into their storytelling and forget to focus on other customers who are probably more likely to purchase something. Expressive people tend to be self-centered, so when engaged with them, keep the focus on them and their needs and desires. They will love you for it.

3. You would think that a **"Solid"** person would be strong and sure in their convictions. Quite the opposite is true.

These people have tremendous difficulty choosing and making up their minds. Solids will take a <u>long</u> time to decide, if they ever do. They usually bring a friend or family member, or sometimes even an entourage with them to help them make decisions.

If alone, they will call someone or even ask YOU to help them decide. They may leave and come back several times, just trying to figure out if they should buy something or not.

Even after they decide, even after they purchase something and drive away, they may change their minds and come back to return the item.

(NOTE: This rarely happens. However, if people do come back later to return items, it is important to tell them kindly, yet firmly, that all sales are final and returns are not accepted due to limited selling time.)

Solids will usually ask you to tell them everything you know about an item, in great detail, and ask LOTS of questions. Your role is that of a guidance counselor. Be soft, kind, patient, and loving with them.

However, these people do tend to take up a lot of time, so if you feel their questions about a $1 item are keeping you from speaking to another customer who is looking at your $300 sofa for sale, excuse yourself politely and either send over one of your helpers to continue the conversation or say you will be back to help them once you have fewer customers. They usually don't mind waiting.

4. **"Analytical"** people will be extremely detail oriented and may even show up with a clipboard for note taking. They will ask you serious questions, and have no time for trivial chatter. They only want to talk about the item, and if you don't know absolutely everything about it, they probably won't trust you.

If you don't know how to answer one of their questions, apologize for not knowing, and be proactive in finding an answer for them as quickly as possible. They will appreciate your interest in helping them.

These people will purchase easily if they can readily see or learn the quality and value of an item. The more reasons you give them about why the item has quality and value for their money, the more likely they will be to purchase it.

Speak in a calm, serious, detailed, intellectual manner to Analyticals, and they will respond well to your languaging.

So now you have learned a shortened version of the DESA system. The more you practice these techniques, the more they will come to you naturally. They are actually great for all relationships, not just sales!

Another advanced sales secret is to quickly determine if a person is more visual, oral, or emotional.

An **Expressive**, for example, is usually visual and effusive about how something looks. Therefore, it makes more sense to say things like, "I **see** what you are saying" to them rather than "I hear what you saying," or "I understand what you are saying."

Choose "I **hear** what you are saying" for a **Dominant** or an **Analytical**," as the first type enjoys telling others what he or she knows, and the second will ask lots of questions to get as much information about an item as possible.

With a **Solid**, choose "I **understand** what you are saying," as these people tend to operate from their emotions and feelings, so you are speaking their language.

****

I hope this bonus information is helpful for your garage sales... and your life! I wish you great success in <u>everything</u> you do.

GRATITUDE

This book would never have been possible without:

- ✦ my amazing Mom, who began teaching me how to wait on customers in her shop when I was eight years old
- ✦ all the wonderful friends and family members who gave of their valuable time to help with my garage sales through the years
- ✦ various employers in my life who taught me additional sales techniques
- ✦ all my neighbors, who never complained, and many of whom actually joined in the festivities
- ✦ all the customers who purchased so much at my sales, often coming back year after year, and
- ✦ my beloved sister Suzi, who has been a constant support and cheerleader for my successes in life.

I would also like to mention my gratitude to be living in an age where so many free online forums for advertising exist, and for the wonder of online publishing, so that all of us with valuable information to share may do so easily.

With love and gratitude to all, Kathy ♥♥♥

38673411R00040

Made in the USA
Lexington, KY
20 January 2015